CHIC
SIMPLE ®
Components

"Professionals built the *Titanic,* amateurs built the ark."

ANONYMOUS

CHIC
SIMPLE ®
Components

T O O L S

621.9

L897

CCL

ALFRED A. KNOPF   NEW YORK 1994

THIS IS A BORZOI BOOK
PUBLISHED BY ALFRED A. KNOPF, INC.

Copyright © 1994 by Chic Simple,
a partnership of
A Stonework, Ltd., and Kim Johnson Gross, Inc.

KIM JOHNSON GROSS   JEFF STONE

WRITTEN BY ROBERT LOVE
PHOTOGRAPHS BY JAMES WOJCIK
ILLUSTRATIONS BY GREGORY NEMEC
STYLED BY EVE ASHCRAFT

ART DIRECTION BY WAYNE WOLF
ICON ILLUSTRATION BY ERIC HANSON

Library of Congress Cataloging-in-Publication Data
Love, Robert.
Tools/ [written by Robert Love : edited by Kim Johnson Gross
and Jeff Stone].
p. cm. — (Chic simple components)
ISBN 0-679-43223-X
1. Tools. I. Gross, Kim Johnson. II. Stone, Jeff. III. Title. IV. Title: Chic simple
tools. V. Series.
TJ1195.L68 1994
621.9—dc20
94-34450
CIP

Printed and bound in Canada

CONTENTS

"The more you know, the less you need."

AUSTRALIAN ABORIGINAL SAYING

Chic Simple is a primer for living well but sensibly. It's for those who believe that quality of life comes not in accumulating things, but in paring down to the essentials. Chic Simple enables readers to bring value and style into their lives with economy and simplicity.

T O O L S

Whether made of stone or silicone, our tools stand by, waiting for our command (unless you loaned them to someone). They are extensions of human will, the off-spring of human intelligence. By the time we grasp a tool, it already knows what to do—it's been programmed and refined specifically for the task at hand. If we just choose the right tool and get ourselves out of the way, the nail will be sunk, the screw turned, the picture hung, the house built. That's if we choose the right one. If...

> "A tool knows exactly how it is meant to be handled, while the user of the tool can only have an approximate idea."
>
> MILAN KUNDERA

THE HISTORY OF TOOLS
IS THE TIME LINE THAT ARCHAEOLOGISTS

HAVE COME TO USE IN CHARTING THE PROGRESS OF HUMAN civilization. By studying the kinds of tools they turn up they have a reading of what the early homeowner was up to. And what better indicator of how we are faring on earth than the things we use to shape it to our liking? In the earliest pages of our history, we huddled in smoky caves and carved a flinty existence from bone and rock. The Bronze Age gave the green light to urban existence and to the first use of pure metals as cutting tools. By 3500 B.C. metal casting was common in the Middle East; by 1100 B.C., in the New World. The Iron Age started with the Egyptians, who were hammering iron before 1350 B.C. The Industrial Age took the workbench and added power—first steam, then electricity. Now we are cordless and neon-colored, and—happily for future generations—the possessors of duct tape.

"Any sufficiently advanced technology is indistinguishable from magic."

ARTHUR C. CLARKE

TOOLING AROUND

"All the tools we use today," wrote Umberto Eco and Giovanni Battista Zorzoli in their Picture History of Inventions, *"are based on things made in the dawn of prehistory."* Like the common handsaw, which our Neanderthal ancestors came up with—a flint-toothed model—some 130,000 years ago. By **10 B.C.** the chisel was in common use in the Middle East, and by **50 B.C.** the first plane with a wood body and metal blade appeared in shops. The Greeks invented the screw; the Romans had a version of the claw hammer. By the **13th CENTURY** the Chinese had invented sandpaper by sticking crushed seashells onto parchment. The rest was all a matter of refinement and automation. Around **1900** the powered circular saw was invented in England. In **1914** the portable electric drill was invented. In **1987** the rechargeable cordless electric screwdriver hit the market.

13

Hand Tools. For jobs requiring precision and touch, nothing is better than the human hand, holding the appropriate tool, guided by an expert eye and the wisdom of experience. Among fine craftsmen, there is a school of thought which says that one should develop an expertise with manual tools before acquiring any power tool, just as pedaling the bicycle comes before driving the car. Any basic tool kit, then, should start with hand tools, a few at a time, until necessity calls for specialization and power. Learning to control these simple tools will pay off. "Things men have made with wakened hands," wrote D. H. Lawrence, "and put soft life into…go on glowing for long years."

> "Basically, a tool is an object that enables you to take advantage of the laws of physics and mechanics in such a way that you can seriously injure yourself."
>
> DAVE BARRY

Power Tools. Like Prometheus taking fire from the gods, we plug our tools into the wall socket and bring to our labors a powerful collaborator. Dull, repetitive work fuels the imagination of tool engineers, and so for every task that would tire a human hand—sanding a door, cutting enough redwood planks to construct an outdoor deck—there is a powered solution that works at dozens, hundreds, or thousands of revolutions a minute. But as with hand tools, patience and control are important factors—even more so at 110 or 220 volts—and their absence will open a Pandora's box of calamities. A gouged wooden floor or a crooked screw hole is the shameful evidence of haste.

SMOOTH OPERATOR. *The palm sander, a versatile finishing tool for wood and a few other soft materials, turns at 10,000 orbital revolutions a minute. It's a willing slave to the grind, but don't bear down on it, and move it with the grain. The coarseness or fineness of the finish will be determined not by the machine, but by the type of sandpaper that's affixed to the sander's metal jaws.*

"Sattinger's Law:
It works better if you
plug it in."

ARTHUR BLOCH

PALM SANDER

Ergonomics. How the tool fits the hand is a relatively recent concern. Where once handles were necessarily rigid, they are now contoured for comfort, ribbed for a tighter grip. With the development of metal-hard moldable resins, many new tools can retain or even increase their tensile strength and still be used comfortably for long periods. The best screwdrivers, for instance, match handle size to blade size for balance, add a cushioned handle, and sometimes even a top that spins in your palm to prevent your hand from cramping up and falling off.

CUTTING EDGE. *Jack-of-all-trades, the utility knife, with its razor-sharp edge, can cut Sheetrock, mark off a thirty-second of an inch on wood, trim wallpaper, or even scrape paint from a windowpane. Utility knives come in two basic varieties—with fixed or retractable blades—but either way it is the replaceable high-carbon steel blade that provides the appropriate magic for the application. Replacement blades, sometimes stored in the handle of the case, can be hooked or curved, as thin as .017 inches for a light, general-duty blade, or as thick as .031 inches for the parrot-beaked linoleum cutter. The newest variation is the brightly colored plastic version with a long blade that snaps off in segments to provide a sharp new cutting edge in a flash.*

Leverage. Most tools take their genetic code from the lever (one of the six so-called simple machines, the others being the wedge, wheel and axle, pulley, screw, and inclined plane). The simple lever, remember, is a mechanical device that uses a small rock (fulcrum) and a board to move a larger rock that couldn't be lifted otherwise. The guiding principle, known as LEVERAGE, is all about easing the work by multiplying energy through the use of distance, which is why a longer lever will more easily raise the rock and why a longer screwdriver allows the human arm to generate more torque, or rotating power. The same is true of your car's lug wrench, as anyone who has tried to change a flat tire can tell you. But a length of pipe slipped over the wrench will provide you with a larger lever and an easier time on the side of the road.

"Give us the tools, and we will finish the job."

WINSTON CHURCHILL

Simple Tools. Sometimes a single tool can take on a multiplicity of tasks. Look no further than the jackknife for a perfect example of this kind of utility. In a pinch, it can turn a screw, poke a hole, cut a rug, fish out a wire, and carve out a nation. Likewise, anyone armed with just a few good tools, will find a way to get most jobs done with what's at hand. Which brings us to the near-at-hand, minimum-requirement kitchen-drawer tool kit that every home deserves. What should be in it? A jackknife or utility knife, of course, and also a small tack hammer and spirit level for hanging pictures. A set of screwdrivers and an adjustable wrench will help you assemble any child's toy. Add a pair of cutting pliers to snip speaker wires, scissors, twine, a jar of nails, screws, tacks, a tape measure, and a flashlight.

"The hardest knife ill-used doth lose his edge."

WILLIAM SHAKESPEARE

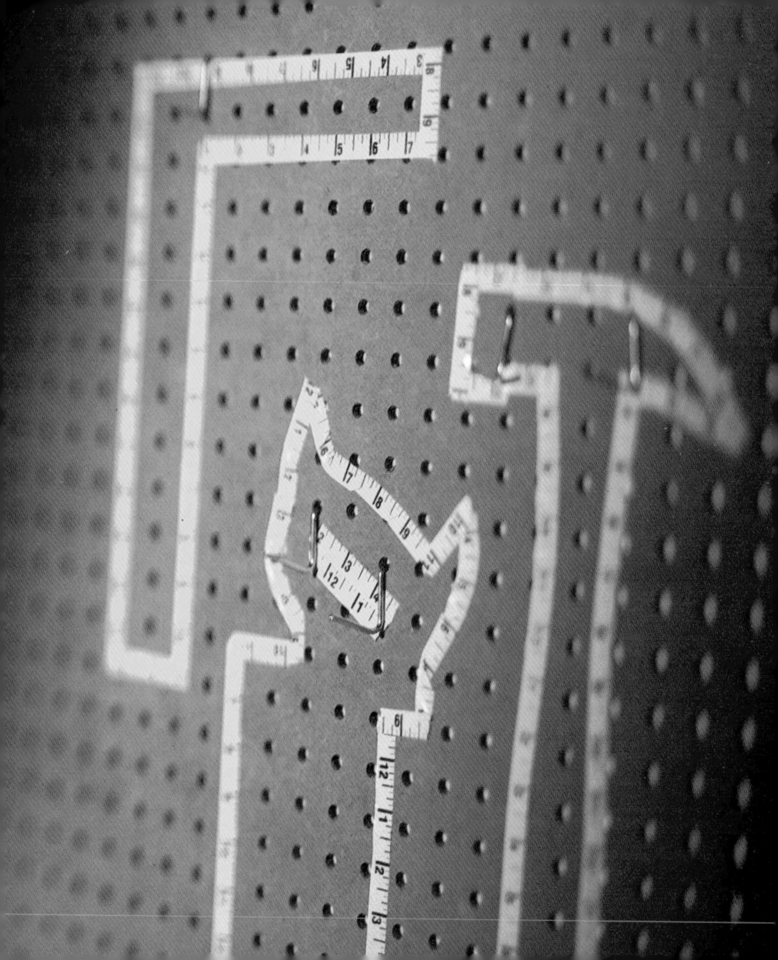

B A S I C S

Next, one by one, the tools that measure and mark, that cut, fasten, and finish. Each is pure in its simplicity, time-tested in its design. Nearly all the sophisticated crafts-men's techniques, from carpentry to plumbing, grow out of the mastery of these few. As Robert Pirsig wrote in *Zen and the Art of Motorcycle Maintenance*, good tools, as a rule, don't wear out. Acquire these good tools first—chosen correctly, they will become life partners.

"The first rule of intelligent tinkering
is to save all the parts."

PAUL R. EHRLICH

Hammers. One of the

most ancient of implements and a

mainstay of any basic kit, the hammer comes in

a dizzying variety of sizes and types. All hammers are

alike in that they consist of a striking surface and a handle.

Hammers are sold by weight, specifically the weight of the head,

which gives a relative idea of the striking power of the tool. The heavier the head the greater the striking force hitting the target. Handles, the cheap and replaceable part of the hammer, are described by length. Find one with a wood or fiberglass handle that feels controllable in your grip when you grasp it at the end. It's not a good idea to choke up on the handle for control; find a lighter hammer instead.

CLAW

FRAMING
HAMMER

HEAD

BAD VIBES
Avoid metal handles in hammers.
They produce vibrations that
tire your arm.

"If I had a hammer..."

TRADITIONAL FOLK SONG

CURVED OR CLAW   **TACK**   **BALL PEEN**   **STRAIGHT**

HAMMER TIME. *The* **CLAW HAMMER**, *the most common of this quartet of pounders, has a forged steel head attached to a wooden or fiberglass handle and is used primarily to drive nails into wood. The peen end of this hammer (that's the opposite of the striking end) is curved for pulling nails. A* **STRAIGHT CLAW HAMMER** *is designed for hammering and prying apart wood, useful for demolition or just for opening wooden crates. A* **TACK HAMMER**, *compact and light, is perfect for driving small nails, brads, or picture hangers. The* **BALL PEEN HAMMER**, *with its case-hardened head, pounds cold chisels and punches and is also used to shape metal.*

1 5/8-INCH
BLACK PANEL NAIL

2-INCH
FINISHING NAIL

1 1/2-INCH
COMMON NAIL

1 1/4 x 16
BRAD

1/16-INCH
BLUE STEEL
TACK

3/8-INCH
U TACK

ALUMINUM
ROOFING NAIL

3-INCH
MASONRY NAIL

NAILED. *Nails are sold by size, finish, and function—for openers, anyway. You'll also see them referred to by pennyweight, which is the way they were sold years ago, when ten cents bought 100 three-inch nails. For now, however, it's better to consult the chart in the hardware store or tell the clerk exactly what job you want the nail to do. For an outdoor-mailbox project, get galvanized or rust-resistant nails. For tacking on a baseboard molding, ask for finishing nails, whose small heads are designed to be driven beneath the surface of the wood with a nail set for a neat appearance. And the general rule for length is: Use a nail two and a half times as thick as the piece you are nailing.*

Saws. Watch the teeth: they tell the saw's story. The more teeth per inch, the finer the cut. Check out the wood; see which way the grain runs. Then choose your weapon. CROSSCUT SAWS, so named because they cut across the grain of a piece of wood, generally have ten to twelve teeth per inch. RIPSAWS, which cut with the grain—think of it cutting along the length of a board—have square teeth at five or six per inch. Both of these, like all American handsaws, cut on the downstroke. To use a crosscut saw correctly, place the saw to the outside of the mark and pull up slightly once or twice, guiding with your thumb, to open a channel in the wood. Then begin sawing slowly and evenly, adding a bit more power on the downstroke. If you are buying only one, purchase the crosscut. A saw is only as efficient as the sharpness of its teeth. Most dullness in a usual home situation is not from use but bad storage. The teeth guard the saw comes with, usually cardboard, sometimes plastic, should be saved and kept on when the saw isn't in use.

RIPSAW

CROSSCUT
SAW

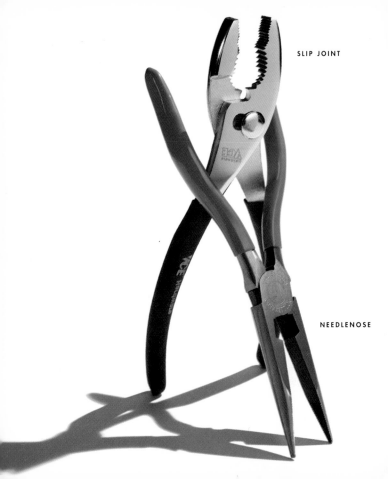

SLIP JOINT

NEEDLENOSE

Pliers. To have and to hold, and also to tighten, turn, squeeze, or pluck—these are some of the assignments for the pliers, an essential component for the toolbox. Pliers come in a variety of sizes related to the work they must perform, but in only two basic types: SOLID JOINT and SLIP JOINT, the latter being a fancy term for pliers with adjustable jaws. Pliers are meant to hold things tightly, most often metal bolts or nuts. Be careful, though: pliers can round the edges of nuts—an adjustable wrench is the proper tool for the job. Some pliers come with a cutting edge for snipping—everything from lamp wire to packing bands. The best pliers are forged from fine-grained steel, with hand-honed surfaces. Their grips are covered in a rubberized plastic (but are never guaranteed to be shockproof). A sensible choice for a first round of tool buying would be these three: a SIX-INCH SLIP JOINT for general duty, a pair of medium NEEDLENOSE pliers for fine work—on jewelry, eyeglasses, electronics—and a pair of DIAGONALS, which have small, sharp cutting heads designed to bite through metals.

Screwdrivers. It's the screws that have passed down their names to their drivers: slotted-head or Phillips, or perhaps the more exotic Torx and square drive, and by those names we know them. Though the screwdriver does only one thing very well, it has benefited, perhaps more than most tools, from late-twentieth-century technology. Now screwdrivers can be

PHILLIPS HEAD

found with contoured, bulb-like handles in neon colors (so you don't leave them in a corner) or magnetic tips to fish out errant screws. They come sized by length (which includes the handle) and generally with a proportioned blade. The most important thing to know here is that size counts: match the screwdriver closely to the size of the screw and the rest is easy.

SLOTTED-HEAD

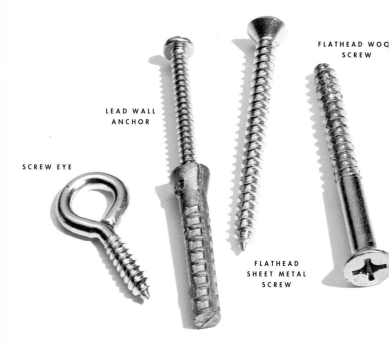

FLATHEAD WOOD
SCREW

LEAD WALL
ANCHOR

SCREW EYE

FLATHEAD
SHEET METAL
SCREW

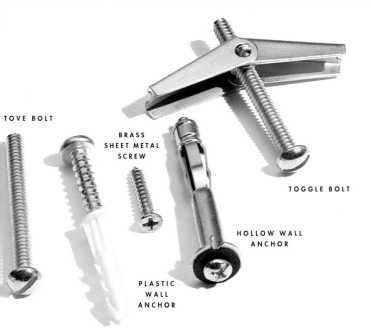

TOVE BOLT

**BRASS
SHEET METAL
SCREW**

TOGGLE BOLT

**HOLLOW WALL
ANCHOR**

**PLASTIC
WALL
ANCHOR**

THE TURN OF THE SCREW. *Where do they go? The answer is, everywhere you need attachments. If you're putting in a door hinge or a switch plate, opening the top of your computer or trying to fix a vacuum cleaner, you'll encounter screws. Like nails, they are sold by size, finish, and function, but their heads (see above) are infinitely more interesting. Some are made for driving into metal (screws that are threaded all the way to the top), and some into wood. Anchors, which are used to attach things to walls, come in several varieties. The lead wall anchor is best for plaster walls and the toggle bolt is meant for hollow walls. Remember, when you unscrew the bolt, the toggle falls down behind the wall—don't feel stupid, it's gravity.*

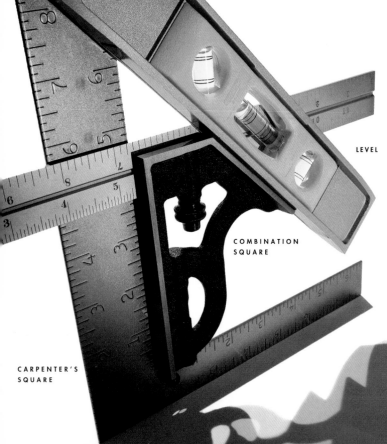

LEVEL

COMBINATION
SQUARE

CARPENTER'S
SQUARE

Straight and Level. These tools are in constant search of the truth: the truly square bookcase, the perfectly level framed photograph. The CARPENTER'S SQUARE, a steel or aluminum L-shaped device, is placed smack against two joined pieces, like the top and sides of a bookcase. Place the pieces together; if no light shows through, the angle is true. The COMBINATION SQUARE, which resembles a steel ruler with a sliding attachment, can also be used to square up joints, or to measure the depth of a hole or mark a 45° angle for joining wall moldings perfectly. The LEVEL, usually a two- or four-foot piece of aluminum or steel, is placed on a surface—for instance, a new stove —to see if it's on the straight and level. Also called a spirit level because the brain of the level is a tiny vial of liquid in which a single bubble floats and the liquid is alcohol(shaken, not stirred). When the level is placed on a surface, watch the bubble: if it floats to a position between the two markings on the vial's glass, the piece is indisputably level.

CARPENTER'S RULE

Use the folding carpenter's rule for measuring inside jobs like a doorjamb or windowsill, for which it is ideal because of its graduated brass extension. Carpenter's rules generally snap out to six feet.

TAPE MEASURE

For longer measuring jobs, take the tape measure, please. The best ones are an inch wide and hold their rigidity over twenty feet, which is a plus when you're working alone and don't have a helper to hold the other end.

Drills. Okay, listen up. Here's the drill: They come in cordless, rechargeable, reversible, and variable-speed models. They're improved every year, and they should have a place in every household. Drills are measured by their chuck size (the round metal part that accepts the drill bit), and the most useful ones measure either ⅜ inch or ½ inch. (The smaller one will do for most chores.) Besides drilling holes, the drill will, with the proper, easily obtained bits and attachments, drive screws, sand wood, grind metal, and even mix paint. But best of all, it drills holes, and everybody likes using it.

UNPLUGGED

A direct descendant of Archimedes' screw, the hand-powered drill was used by generations of carpenters to drill straight and perfect holes. It still has a place in a complete tool kit, too. If you're making one or two holes, the setup for this drill takes half the time, and the result is the same. Why waste 2,500 rpm's and all those watts on a task that requires a couple of turns of the handle?

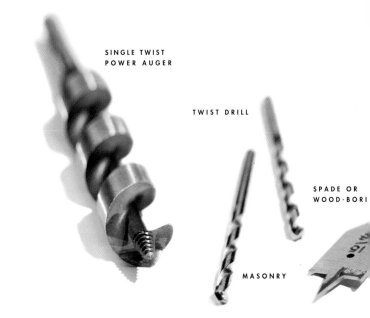

SINGLE TWIST
POWER AUGER

TWIST DRILL

SPADE OR
WOOD-BORI

MASONRY

DRILL TEAM. *A drill, no matter how fast it's spinning, is nothing without the bit—the thing that actually bores the hole. Bits come in a variety of sizes and in special applications to match the material that's getting the hole drilled into it. Twist drills, the most common, have channels cut into them for removing debris when drilling, and are used on metal and wood. A spade bit, with its flat cutting edge, is used on wood only. Masonry bits feature a tungsten tip for driving through concrete and plaster. Countersink bits leave a wider space near the top of the hole; when a screw is driven in, the screwhead sinks below the surface. And stop collars ensure that the bits always reach a predetermined depth.*

MASONRY OR
PLASTER

COUNTERSINK

DRILL STOP COLLARS
OR STOP COLLARS

CARBIDE TIP
MASONRY

CARPENTER'S PENCIL

SCRATCH AWL

Marking. Before a repair project gets started, things must be quietly measured and accurately marked. Though marking might seem to the uninitiated like a no-brainer, there's more science to it than one might think. The carpenter's pencil, with its flat case (so that it doesn't roll away) is fine for rough jobs, but not at tolerances of less than a sixteenth of an inch. More precise measurements need a finer point; many craftsmen like to use a sharp draftsman's pencil. A scriber, or scratch awl, which resembles an ice pick, is designed to cut a visible scratch across wood and other material. And don't overlook the utility knife, which can scribe an extremely fine line.

MARK MY WORDS
A short list of things that should be marked first:
1. A replacement shelf for an old closet **2.** *A new piece of chair-rail molding* **3.** *The height of a bulletin board* **4.** *The depth of a cabinet* **5.** *The right spot for drapery hardware* **6.** *The pieces of a simple homemade window box*

LIPSTICK TRACES
When you need to mark cutouts in sheets of material—like an outlet box in the middle of a sheet of wallboard— measuring can take forever. A down-and-dirty trick is to rub lipstick on the edge of the box and then press the sheet against it.

Bucket Brigade. A five-gallon plastic bucket, outfitted with this ingenious jacket (it's called a Bucket Buddy) turns into a lightweight, movable tool carrier. Bring it with you to your workshop and then take a minute to figure out exactly what you'll need to carry to the task at hand. This process will help you mentally map out the job ahead, and cut down on the number of trips back to the toolbox.

"There are three ways to get something done: do it yourself, hire someone, or forbid your kids to do it."

MONTA CRANE

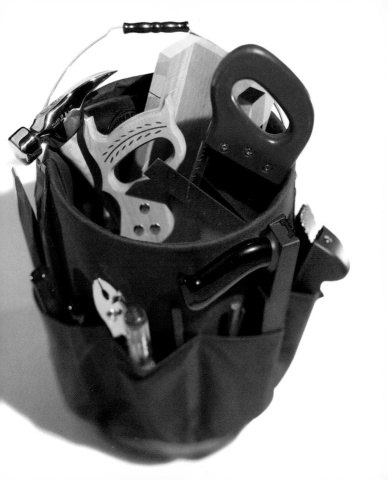

BEYOND BASICS

The first rule is: Always use the right tool. A big, beautiful screwdriver won't turn a simple little screw. Likewise, the most powerful wrench may not exactly fit where you want it to go. The challenge is not just to have the right tool in your possession but to have it at the ready. We move now beyond the basics into more specialized terrain, where the tasks are unique and the tools are, too.

"I love buying expensive power
tools and using them to wreck various parts
of my house."

DAVID OWEN

CURVED JAW
VISE-GRIP®

NEEDLENOSE
VISE-GRIP®

Locking Pliers. Like Kleenex tissues and the Windbreaker jacket, Vise-Grips ® have become part of the mechanical *lingua franca* as the synonym for locking pliers. Patented by the American Tool Company in 1924, Vise-Grips ®, as well as their generic identical twins, are the versatile tool to turn to when you need a third hand to grip a pipe or a nut—a situation that often arises while doing home-plumbing repairs, like detaching a drainpipe or replacing old faucets. (A pair of locking pliers will also double as a simple clamp if needed.) Though they open and close like standard pliers, Vise-Grips ® feature an adjustable jaw controlled by a screw in the bottom of one side of the handle. Once the jaws are adjusted to the desired size, these pliers squeeze down and hang on, leaving both your hands free to tighten or turn. When the job is done, the pressure is released by moving a lever on the side of the handle. Locking pliers come in various sizes, with straight or curved edges and in "needlenose" varieties, but a medium-sized seven-inch pair should suffice for most tasks.

BLOCK PLANE

Planes. Planes are used on wood, to trim or shape it, to clean up the rough edges and splinters left behind by a saw or a drill, and generally to provide a smooth surface ready for sanding and finishing. In the hands of an experienced user, a plane responds more sensitively than any powered machine to the slightest increase in pressure. Every plane has a steel blade and an adjusting mechanism that determines

SURFORM
POCKET BLADE

SURFORM
PLANE

SURFORM
SHAVER

the angle of the cut. The BLOCK PLANE, made in adjustable and non-adjustable models, is the typical home version, useful for small, light jobs like dressing the ends of cut wood. SURFORMS, surface forming tools, can have plane-type blades or cut like rasps with cheese-grater-type surfaces that will quickly shape wood, plastic, or soft metal, and are especially effective in giving a nice finish to the ends of Sheetrock.

TACK HAMMER

COPING SAW

NAIL SET

CARPENTER'S MALLET

Woodworking.

Perhaps the most beautiful of all specialty tools are the antique-looking mallets, chisels, planes, and other implements of the woodworker. These tools are, by comparison to those in the home toolbox, delicate and expensive. The payoff lies in their ability to master the details and precise measurements of cabinetry. The CHISELS are sharp and designed to take the blows of a wooden

CABINET SCREWDRIVER

SPOKESHAVE

MARKING GAUGE

CARPENTER'S MALLET, (never a metal-headed hammer). The NAIL SET, a pointed punch, is placed on the head of a finishing nail to sink it beneath the surface of the wood, where it is hidden even better with a dab of wood-colored putty. The CABINET SCREWDRIVER has a straight instead of tapered blade to prevent scarring counterbored (sunken) screwholes. A SPOKESHAVE'S HERITAGE (and name) comes from shaving wagon wheel spokes; nowadays, it is used as a plane for fine work.

CIRCULAR SAW BLADES

Combination blade, for hard or soft wood

For cutting meta[l]

Carbide tip, for masonry and brick

Fine-toothed, fo[r] plywood

Fast-cut crosscuts, for wood

Splinter-free combination blade for various materials

Power Saw. Its 2-horsepower motor whirling at some 5,000 revolutions per minute, the circular saw can make rapid cuts through lumber, masonry, even metals, if equipped with the appropriate blade. As with handsaws, the greater number of teeth, the finer the cut, and the finest is reserved for plywood, which splinters easily. Combination blades can handle ripping and cross-cutting through hard and soft woods. Circular saw blades are sold in several diameters, but 7 1/4-inch blades are the most common.

Plumb Bob. Other tools fight gravity and inertia, but the infallible plumb bob goes with the flow—and provides correct results every time. An ancient measuring device, the plumb bob consists of two parts, a coarse string or cord, and a weight attached to one end. Suspend it from any point, and the plumb bob, when it stops swaying, will show you what is truly vertical, or plumb. (It stands to reason: a string held down by a weight would have to be a straight line.) The Incas used the plumb bob to build the city of Machu Picchu, and there is evidence that the Egyptians used it to build perfect pyramids. You, however, can use the plumb bob to determine if the studs you're nailing up to support a drywall are straight or leaning; or where the chandelier should be hung if it is to hover directly above the center of the dining room table; or if the doorjamb for which you've cut a hole in the wall will accommodate a door with true angles. You could do these jobs without one, but you may end up plumb out of luck.

Staple Gun. Where tacks and hammers and bloody cuticles once ruled, now the staple gun is king. Whether it's a spring-loaded delivery system—the most common and economical model for home use—or an electric model, or a more expensive hammer stapler, which releases a staple on impact, the staple gun is a twentieth-century device that's perfect for such modern tasks as laying carpet, attaching fabrics to wood for window treatments or upholstery, affixing ceiling tiles, drawer liners, or insulation. The staple gun is really just a brawnier version of the desk model, but its staples range in depth from $1/4$ inch to $9/16$ inch and the power with which they are delivered should be apparent enough to instill a measure of caution in the careful user. Hint: Look for models made of sturdy lightweight plastic that will accept two different sizes of staples on sliding-tray loading systems. Newer models also have driving devices that minimize recoil, which can quickly tire the unsuspecting hand.

WIRE CUT▶

MULTI-PLIERS

Electrical. It's all around us, but we never see it; instead, we see its effects. The tools of the electrician are designed to direct this powerful, invisible force so that it does its work silently and harmlessly. Like stripping wires. You strip wire in order to expose it before connecting it to something else, probably another wire. **WIRE STRIPPERS**, at left, come with a variety of wire gauges. Just find the right one, snip, and twist. Any tool that may come into contact with electricity should have a set of rubberized grips. Even so, tool companies will make no claim that their tools are shockproof, so ultimately it's smarter and safer to go over to the fuse box or switch and make sure the juice is off.

SOLDERING GUN
Like life, soldering is all about connections and flux. You use a soldering gun to create a metallic anchor for electrical leads. Turn it on. When the tip of the gun is sufficiently heated, feed it the solder, which is an alloy of lead and tin with a very low melting point. As the solder heats up and turns to molten silver, watch it flow like magic to the places where you've dabbed the flux. After it cools, the connection is hard and durable.

Digital. The digital revolution has yet to make great advances into the home toolbox, but that's not to say that the computer has no business there. Just walk into the cache of a well-stocked auto mechanic and you'll see a vast array of digital diagnostic devices, from oscilloscopes to timing lights, tach dwell meters, thermometers, and volt

ON/OFF

SMARTLEVEL®

"Build me straight

meters. An electrician, naturally, will have a digital device or two. And now here's something for the carpenter who has everything: an electronic, battery-powered level with a digital readout. Great for making anything true, and trying to get the digital readout to center is a fun sort of Zen party game. I'm centered, you're not—mantra city.

DIGITAL LEVEL

) worthy Master!"

HENRY WADSWORTH LONGFELLOW

"The Building of the Ship," 1850

"Put your toys away."

MOM

THE TEN
COMMANDMENTS

(plus one)

1. Thou shalt keep tools dry, away from moisture and dampness.

2. Thou shalt keep them organized, for any task that requires a tool cannot be be begun until that tool is found.

3. Thou shalt unplug all electrical tools after you use them and keep them far from little hands.

4. Thou shalt assign a permanent place to each tool that you acquire, when you acquire it, so that thou shalt never have to devote a Saturday morning to a full-scale organization of them.

5. Thou shalt take the occasional Saturday morning off to organize your toolbox because you'll fail to heed the Fourth Commandment.

6. Thou shalt stay focused on thy task while using power tools and never simultaneously discuss money or family with thy mate.

7. Thou shalt check thy measurement—once, twice, thrice—and be sure the lumber store is still open before cutting.

8. Thou shalt loan thy tools but never out of thy sight.

9. Thou shalt never demonstrate to thy spouse how to use tools.

10. Thou shalt only buy what is on thy list upon visiting the hardware store—no more, no less.

11. Thou shalt return to the hardware store the duplicate tool thou bought because of not heeding the previous commandment.

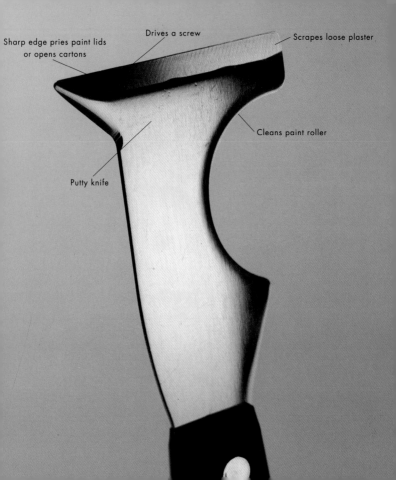

Sharp edge pries paint lids
or opens cartons

Drives a screw

Scrapes loose plaster

Cleans paint roller

Putty knife

Five-in-One. To devotees of tools, combination devices—
at least those that combine more than two or three functions—
are the lovable freaks of the workbench. Some, like the Swiss
Army knife, have always commanded a certain amount of respect
for the sheer achievement of cramming all those blades and
drivers, along with a toothpick, into a slim red case. Others,
like the Bit Kit, a modular screwdriver set that comes with a
variety of interchangeable tips to fit the increasing variety of
screwheads, have won respect through field use. The dirty little secret of most three-, four-, or five-in-one tools is that they
don't do any one thing exceedingly well. Nevertheless, a tool
like this one has won the affection of painters for its ability to
open paint cans, slice open a carton, hammer away loose plaster
from a wall, drive a screw, and—with its curved surface—expert-
ly scrape leftover paint from a roller when the cleanup begins.

"It is well with me only when I have a chisel in hand."

MICHELANGELO

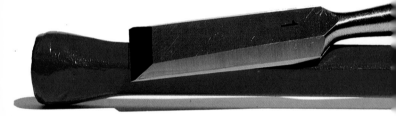

Chisels. The hammer's sedentary sidekick, the chisel, is a shaping tool that uses transferred energy to trim material like wood or metal or stone. But listen closely: They're not all the same. It's essential to know exactly what kind of chisel you're holding. Pounding a WOOD CHISEL against metal will ruin the tool's edge in a moment—as will using it to drive screws or open paint cans. You might use a chisel to break off a rusted bolt on a backyard fence gate. Or you might

COLD CHISEL

STANLEY

Professional™

6 U.S.A.

R GOGGLES

use a different one to chip away an eighth of an inch of wood molding around a switch plate during an attic renovation. On cold cruel metal, use what's called a COLD CHISEL, which has a steel face where it meets the hammer. A chisel will only cut a material softer than itself, so cold chisels, made from steel, will cut cast iron, wrought iron, bronze, copper, etc. Most, but not all, are designed to be whacked on the back with a mallet or a hammer while held in your fist.

Wrenches. The wrencho-deluxe of all fasteners, the gleaming chrome-and-nickel-plated, tempered-steel ADJUSTABLE WRENCH will tighten a toilet seat or loosen a faucet. It comes to the rescue for bike, boat, or car in sizes that run from six inches to a foot. Pick up a well-made adjustable and balance it in your hand. Then thumb the spiral adjustment until the jaws open to the correct size. Now place it over the nut or bolt head and gently pull (never push, unless you absolutely have to) until you feel the leverage overcome its resistance and the nut give way. Don't become addicted to the adjustable, however. It's always better to use the correct combination, box, or open-end wrench if you have it. That will prevent eventual rounding off of the nut or bolt.

1 . Adjustable wrench
2 . Combination wrench, open-end and box end
3 . Open-end wrench

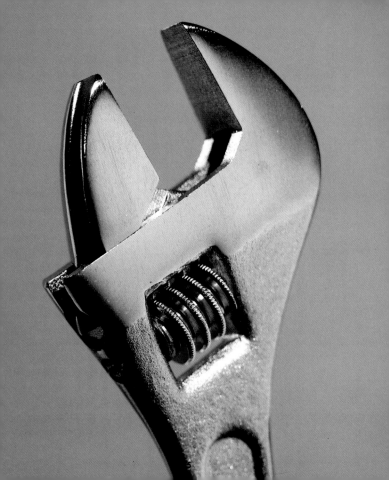

Tool Belts. The things they carry with them tell who they are. The CARPENTER'S TOOL BELT will no doubt have a loop for a hammer, as well as sleeves for a tape measure and a utility knife, and pouches for nails and screws. The ELECTRICIAN'S BELT must allow quick on-site access to his insulated pliers as well as a host of screwdrivers, since he is probably working in more cramped quarters than other craftsmen. For everybody, including do-it-yourselfers, the best tool belts, like holsters, are made of leather, ride off the hips, and are designed for the quick draw when you're sitting atop a ladder. Tool belts come in a variety of weights, with a differing number of pockets, depending on the type of work you're doing. Look for good heavy stitching, metal reinforcements of the seams, and a sturdy webbed belt to buckle it around your waist.

"The hole and the patch should be commensurate."

THOMAS JEFFERSON

RATCHET WRENCHES

SOCKET SCREWDRIVER

SOCKET WRENCH

ALLEN OR
HEX KEY WRENCH

SOCKET SET

Metal to Metal. If you take apart anything even vaguely mechanical, from the lawn mower to that new mountain bike, these are the tools you will need. The mechanic's tools today are thinner, stronger, and better engineered than ever before. The best of this breed are sold by American companies like Stanley and Snap-On, made of cold forged steel, coated with chrome, nickel, and molybdenum and hand polished. Snap-On has improved the torque of the standard box wrench by up to 50 percent. If you want to learn more, follow Robert Pirsig's advice in *Zen and the Art of Motorcycle Maintenance*, "Study the tool catalogs."

"Warning: Do not be misled by advertisements for so-called tool sets allegedly containing large numbers of tools.... Oh, sure, you get a lot of tools, but most of them are the same kind! For example, you'll get 127 wrenches, and the only differences is that one will be maybe an eighth of an inch bigger than another. Big deal."

DAVE BARRY

KEYHOLE SAW
Its thin, pointe[d]
blade will fit i[n]
tight spaces.

Specialty Saws. Once you've taken a few whacks at a pine bookcase with a typical combination household saw, you'll realize that it can't do everything. For angle-cutting moldings and trim in a miter box or on the wall, you'll need the stiff, straight **BACKSAW**. A **KEYHOLE SAW** is a must for putting locksets into doors. And a **COPING SAW** is used for making delicate cuts or curved lines. **HACKSAWS** are finer-toothed, and used to cut metal; they're usually mounted in a fixed frame for extra precision. This saw will handle almost all household jobs involving cutting metals—nails, pipes, bolts, and also weird stuff like plastic and frozen food. It cuts on the push stroke, so ease up on the backstroke.

HACKSAW

COPING SAW
With its thin blade in
a U-shaped holder, it
is used for more delicate
work such as cutting trim
for corners.

BACKSAW
The reinforcing steel
across the top easily
cuts a piece lying flat,
like molding.

HOSE CLAMP

SPRING CLAMP

C-CLAMP

WEB OR BAND CLAMP

Clamps. Wherever togetherness is needed, whether it's permanent or temporary, the clamp comes on strong. For every field of endeavor there are specialty clamps, ingenious in their idiosyncratic nature. Like the HOSE CLAMP, which is used in plumbing to make a watertight connection between a rubber hose and a metal pipe. Just slip it over the tubing and connect by tightening the slotted screw. The all-purpose SPRING CLAMP, like two strong fingers, will hold and hold while you do other things. When space is tight and it seems that no clamp will be small enough to wrap around something, bring out the WEB or BAND CLAMP, which uses a thin, strong mesh belt with a tightening device. And last but not least, the humble C-CLAMP, so named for its C-shaped jaws, which tightens nicely with a T-bar-topped screw. Use the C-clamp primarily for metal-to-metal connections; with proper padding, it can be used with wood.

SLIP-GROOVE
PLIERS OR
CHANNELLOCKS®

STRAP WRENCH

Plumbing. Water is a force as powerful as electricity, but it's one we have tamed. We expect water to appear on command and disappear without further ado. And that's what the plumber's tools guarantee. The PIPE WRENCH, with its pivoted, gripping head, turns the pipe, and the HACKSAW cuts it to the right length. Then

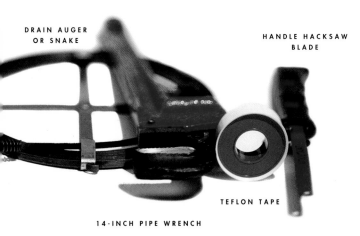

DRAIN AUGER
OR SNAKE

HANDLE HACKSAW
BLADE

TEFLON TAPE

14-INCH PIPE WRENCH

the **PROPANE TORCH** sweats the joined pipes (sweating means heating the joint until the solder flows into the crevices) to preclude any leaks. When the water won't go away, the **DRAIN AUGER** or **SNAKE** forces its way through curved pipe to break up blockages so that water spirals nicely on its way down the drain.

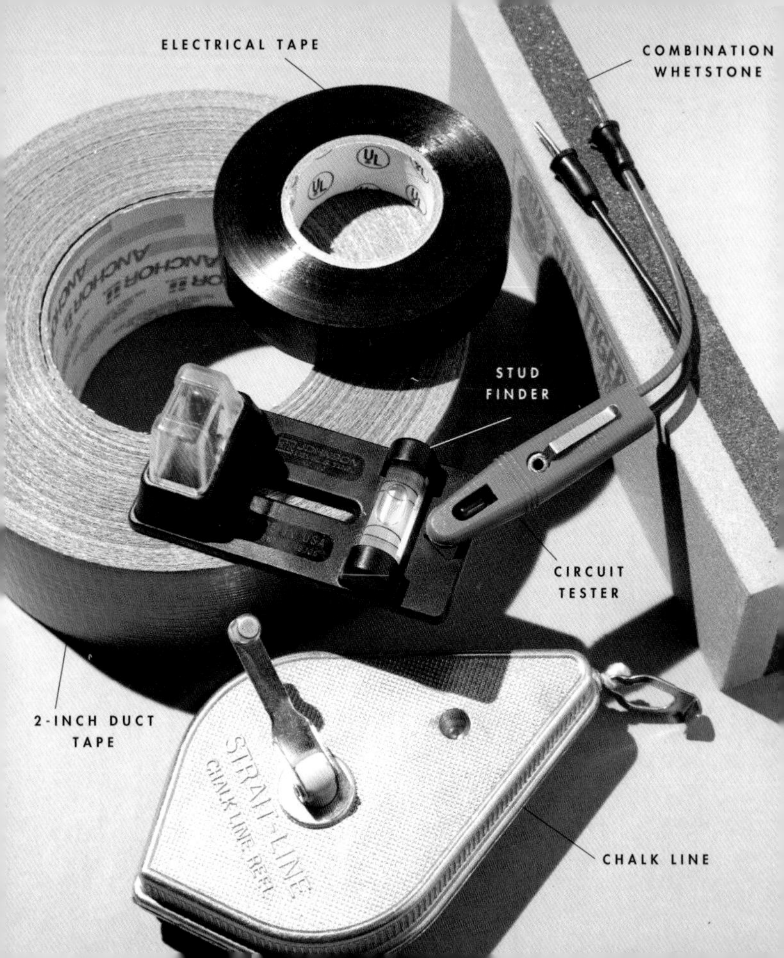

ELECTRICAL TAPE
COMBINATION WHETSTONE
STUD FINDER
CIRCUIT TESTER
2-INCH DUCT TAPE
CHALK LINE
STRAIT-LINE
CHALK LINE REEL

Stuff. These are the extra items that may not seem worth the money at first, but which turn out to be necessities. Whoever invented strong, fibrous DUCT TAPE should get a MacArthur grant—the stuff does a million sticky jobs well, from closing gaps when an air conditioner doesn't fit a window to mending car or boat upholstery (at least temporarily). ELECTRICAL TAPE, on the other hand, does a single task very well—it covers, insulates, and protects bare or exposed electrical wire; it should never be used for mundane jobs like sealing cartons. When a straight line needs to be marked over a long distance, bring out the CHALK LINE. Pull the string from the metal case and hold it taut between two points. Give it a snap and *voilà:* a sharp-edged line in colored chalk. The STUD FINDER takes the guesswork out of finding the right place to attach nails or screws for shelves. A WHETSTONE keeps the edges of cutting tools sharp, and a CIRCUIT TESTER, when plugged into electrical connections, wall sockets, or appliances, tells you whether the juice is flowing.

Toolbox Logic. The best tool-and-owner relationships are marked by stability and commitment. Give your tools a permanent, sturdy home, and in return they will be waiting there to serve you. How often are we interrupted at the crucial moment when nail and hammer are to meet because, well, hammer is nowhere to be found. The organized toolbox saves us from such frustration. A multileveled metal storage case has a place for almost everything, and emanates order. Keep big items like hammers and wrenches at the bottom, and the more delicate measuring devices in the long top compartments.

THE WELL-STOCKED TOOLBOX

Once you're past the fear of not knowing what things are called, hardware stores are full of temptation. Just don't make your toolbox too heavy to lift.

LOWER LEVEL

__Hammer
__Saw
__Hacksaw
__Pipe wrench
__Pry bar
__Electric screwdriver
__Cold chisel

MEZZANINE

__C-clamp
__Nuts, bolts, screws, nails
__Nail set
__Extra fuses

TOP LEVEL

__Utility knife
__Wrenches
__Screwdrivers
__Small level
__Carpenter's rule
__Tweezers
__Pencil
__Small flashlight (Maglite)

 # first aid.

The very point of using tools is to accomplish a task while minimizing the effort. Now it's time to employ this book as a tool—one designed to minimize effort when you're working with tools. Read on carefully, and watch your autonomy grow.

MAKE A SAFETY KIT

Assemble a safety kit to go along with (or in or alongside) your toolbox. Make sure you have the following:

1. Fire extinguisher
2. Safety goggles
3. Disposable dust masks
4. Disposable rubber gloves
5. Work gloves
6. Water bottle

METRIC EQUIVALENTS

1 inch	= 25.4 millimeters or 2.54 centimeters
1 foot	= 305 meters
1 meter	= 3.28 feet

EVERYTHING YOU NEED TO KNOW ABOUT NAILS

*To set up a nail for hammering, hold it between your first and second fingers with your **palm turned up** toward you (it hurts less that way if you miss). Grasp the hammer with your other hand—at the end of the handle—and rest it on the nailhead. Bring the hammer back, set the swing, and tap, tap, tap the nailhead straight down. When the nail will stand on its own, raise the hammer back farther and let it drop to the target. Don't swing it or force it—just guide the hammer's head to the nail on gravity's ticket. For best results, hammer nails in at an angle. A stronger joint is usually produced by techniques known as **toenailing** or **dovetail nailing**. To keep a nail from **splintering** a piece of wood, try these* *solutions:* Drill a pilot hole slightly smaller than the nail's diameter and then hammer it in. Or blunt the point of a nail with your hammer. To set a finishing nail, leave about an eighth of an inch showing. Grasp the **nail set** or punch with the fingers and thumb of your free hand and tap it with the hammer until the nail is sunk perhaps a sixteenth of an inch below the surface of the wood. Fill with carpenter's putty and finish.

PENNY FOR YOUR THOUGHTS

Nails are sold by penny size, abbreviated by the use of the letter **d**, an old British system that uses the word **denarius** to mean penny. What this means to you is listed below:

2d = 1 inch	12d = 3.5 inches
4d = 1.5 inches	20d = 4 inches
6d = 2 inches	40d = 5 inches
8d = 2.5 inches	60d = 6 inches
10d = 3 inches	

SCREWS

Screws are sold by length, annotated in inches, as well as diameter, which is described by gauge numbers as well as a number that denotes the number of threads per inch. The two most popular drive heads for screws are still slotted and Phillips in their many variants (screws come in flathead, roundhead, hex head, and other types, although you might run into square drive, Torx, and other more exotic ones).

SCREWY THOUGHTS

What follows below are some common screw sizes.

No. 5 = 1/8 inch	No. 14 = 1/4 inch
No. 6 = 5/32 inch	No. 16 = 17/64 inch
No. 10 = 3/16 inch	No. 24 = 3/8 inch

SINGLE SHINY BOLT LOOKING FOR...

Bolts are threaded rods that fit into nuts. They are sold by length and width or diameter and come in three basic types: carriage bolt, stove bolt, and machine bolt. Of course, they come with corresponding nut sizes.

LUSTY WRENCHES

The choices are not just open-end or box, combination. adjustable, socket, or locking grip. There is a larger question of meter or inches. One company, Snap-On, makes over 1,200 different varieties of wrenches. Choose prepackaged sets of five or six wrenches—one set in metric, the other in inches—and the odds are good that you'll find uses for both.

STRIPTEASE

With the right touch, a pair of diagonals can also double as effective wire strippers. Apply just enough pressure to slit the plastic covering of a wire, then pull.

LUMBER LIES

What you see is not what you get at the lumber store. Lumber is measured first, then milled and dried. Thus a piece of lumber called a two-by-four (or 2 x 4, meaning two inches by four inches) actually measures closer to 1½ inches by 3½ inches. Other common sizes are listed below in inches.

$$1 \times 4 = \text{¾" x 3½"}$$
$$2 \times 6 = \text{1½" x 5½"}$$
$$2 \times 8 = \text{1½" x 7¼"}$$

ROUGH

All power tools throw off vibration, some spew fumes or fling hot, jagged bits of "shrapnel." So be overly careful; use protective eyewear, and if you haven't observed someone with experience use the power tool you're about to plug in, read the instructions twice as carefully. Even professionals say it's always best to try a couple of test runs first.

SAWS

Lubricate the sides (not teeth) of your saw with plain bar soap; it will cut more smoothly. Saws should be hung to avoid damaging their teeth. Long-term storage should include coating the blades lightly with machine oil to prevent rust.

FIVE HELPFUL HOUSEHOLD ITEMS TO HAVE AROUND

*1. **Soap.** Use a bar of soap to get a stubborn screw to go in. Rub the threads across the soap and try again. Running a handsaw's blade across a bar of soap will make cutting wood easier, too.*

*2. **Paper plate.** Tape a paper plate around the bottom of a can of paint to catch spills.*

*3. **Peg-Board.** Besides its utility at the workbench, a Peg-Board can be used to protect decorative trim when it's being installed. Hammer the nail through the hole in the Peg-Board.*

*4. **Hairpin.** If a nail or brad is too small for you to grip it comfortably, use a bobby pin (or small needlenose pliers) to hold it still while you tap with the hammer.*

*5. **Cork.** A common bottle cork can be used as a stopping mechanism on a drill bit to keep it from penetrating too far.*

ONE LAST TIP: SEEK ADVICE

Find a good-quality hardware store and find someone there who will take the time to talk to you. Rules for talking: Don't pretend to know more than you do. Don't be afraid to say what you do know. Wait your turn, describe the results you want, and then seek advice. Good luck; work safely and well.

where. If you can't find what you need

in your toolbox, relax—it's all here. And the only thing more fun than

looking at a book about tools is playing with them in a hardware store.

Even as the world shrinks and chain stores expand globally, there are plenty of locales where choice is limited, if there is any choice at all. However, most manufacturers today can aid you in finding a store or even mail direct to you. The numbers listed below will help give you freedom of choice.

MANUFACTURERS

Black & Decker	410/716-3900
Buck Knives	800/326-2825
Channel Lock	800/724-3018
DeWalt	800/433-9258
Eklind Tool	800/373-1140
Estwing	815/397-9558
Garrett Wade	800/221-2942
Gem Electrics	516/273-2230
Great Neck Source	800/457-0600
Hart Tool Co.	800/331-4495
Hyde Tools	800/872-4933
Johnson Level and Tool	414/242-1161
Klein Tools	800/553-4676
Makita USA	714/522-8088
Millers Falls Tools Co.	513/271-3300

Porter-Cable	800/321-9443
Ridge Tool	216/329-4043
Sandvik Saws & Tools	800/446-7404
SB Power Tool Co.	312/286-7330
Sears Craftsman Club	800/682-8691
Sears Craftman's Tools	800/377-7414
Snap-On Tools	800/866-5749
Stanley Tools	800/262-2161

RETAILERS

Ace Hardware	800/455-4223
Home Depot	800/553-3199
K-Mart	800/635-6278
Radioshack	800/231-3680
ServiStar	412/283-4567
Target	612/370-6073
True Value Hardware	212/517-6300

United States

CALIFORNIA

BAKER'S HARDWARE
3925 San Fernando Road
Glendale, CA 91204
213/245-1945
(Hardware store)

CENTER HARDWARE CO.
999 Mariposa Street
San Francisco, CA 94107
415/861-1800
(Hand tools, hardware)

E. M. HUNDLEY
HARDWARE CO.
617 Bryant Street
San Francisco, CA 94107
415/777-5050
(Builders' hardware, hand tools)

EMPIRE BUILDERS
SUPPLY CO., INC.
1802 Cerrillos Road
San Francisco, CA 94115
415/982-2646
(Hand and power tools)

KOONTZ HARDWARE
8914 Santa Monica
Boulevard
West Hollywood, CA 90069
310/652-0184
(Hardware, tools)

LAUREL HARDWARE
7984 Santa Monica
Boulevard
West Hollywood, CA 90046
213/656-9605
(Hardware, tools)

COLORADO

ALPINE ACE
HARDWARE
300 Puppy Smith Street
Aspen, CO 81611
303/925-3031
(Tools and accessories)

McGUCKIN HARDWARE
2525 Arapahoe
Boulder, CO 80302
303/443-1822
(Tools and power tools)

MINERS BUILDING
319 East Main Street
Aspen, CO 81611
303/925-5550
(Tools and housewares)

RAD HARDWARE AND
HOME CENTER
611 South Broadway
Boulder, CO 80303
303/499-7211
(Tools)

DISTRICT OF COLUMBIA

BROOKLAND
SERVISTAR HARDWARE
3501 12th Street NE
Washington, DC 20017
202/635-3200
(Tools and tools for rent)

DISTRICT SERVISTAR
HARDWARE
1623 17th Street NW
Washington, DC 20009
202/462-3146
(Power and hand tools)

W. T. WEAVER AND
SONS, INC.
1208 Wisconsin Avenue NW
Washington, DC 20007
202/333-4200
(Tools and hardware since 1889)

FLORIDA

ELEGANT HARDWARE,
INC.
6600 West Rogers Circle
Boca Raton, FL 33487
407/736-6611
(Tools, hardware)

MIAMI DISCOUNT
TOOL AND HARDWARE,
INC.
10890 SW 186th Street
Miami, FL 33157
305/235-1553
(Tools)

MOORE'S TRUE VALUE
HARDWARE
10193 Southern Boulevard
West Palm Beach, FL 33411
407/793-0919
(Tools)

MASSACHUSETTS

BROAD STREET
HARDWARE
109 Broad Street
Boston, MA 02110
617/728-4324
(Hand and power tools)

DICKSON BROS. TRUE
VALUE HARDWARE
26 Brattle Street
Cambridge, MA 02138
617/876-6760
(Tools and kitchenware)

MICHIGAN

EAST ANN ARBOR
HARDWARE
3010 Packard Road
Ann Arbor, MI 48108
313/971-5440
(Hand and power tools)

STADIUM HARDWARE
2177 West Stadium
Boulevard
Ann Arbor, MI 48103
313/663-8704
(Hand and power tools)

NEW HAMPSHIRE

RENOVATOR'S SUPPLY
P.O. Box 2515, Dept. 9876
Conway, NH 03818
800/659-2211
*(Lighting, bathroom
hardware)*
Catalog / Mail Order

NEW YORK

CK & L SURPLUS CO.,
INC.
307 Canal Street
New York, NY 10013
212/966-1745
(Retail hardware store)

GARRETT WADE CO.,
INC.
161 Avenue of the Americas
New York, NY 10013
212/807-1155
*(Supplier of fine woodworking
equipment)*

GRACIOUS HOME
1220 and 1217 Third
Avenue
New York, NY 10021
212/517-6300;
212/988-8990
(Hardware, tools)

H. BRICKMAN & SONS
55 First Avenue
New York, NY 10003
212/674-3213
(Paint and hardware store)

JANOVIC/PLAZA, INC.
771 Ninth Avenue
New York, NY 10019
212/245-3241; call for store
locations
*(Paints, hardware, home
supplies)*

METROPOLITAN
LUMBER & HARDWARE
175 Spring Street
New York, NY 10012
212/966-3466
(Hardware and lumber store)

PINTCHIK
278 Third Avenue
New York, NY 10010
212/777-3030 or 212/982-
6600; call for store locations
(Discount home products)

SIMON'S HARDWARE
421 Third Avenue
New York, NY 10016
212/532-9220
(Hardware)

OREGON

ALDERGROVE TRUE
VALUE HARDWARE
16130 Lower Boones Ferry
Road
Lake Oswego, OR 97035
503/636-2425
(Tools)

HIPPO HARDWARE &
TRADING CO.
1040 East Burnside
Portland, OR 97214
503/231-1444
(Hardware, tools)

STANDARD BRANDS
PAINT AND HOME
DECORATING CENTERS
20 NE Hancock
Portland, OR 97212
503/287-8098
(Home accessories and tools)

WINKS HARDWARE
903 NW Davis
Portland, OR 97209
503/227-5536
(Hardware and tools)

NATIONAL LISTING

HOME DEPOT
2727 Paces Ferry Road NW
Atlanta, GA 30339
404/433-8211 or
800/553-3199 for U.S.
listings
(Hardware and tools)

THE LEFT-HANDED
SHOP
57 Brewer Street
W1
71/437-3910
(Tools designed for lefties)

TYLER'S HOMECARE
104-106 Notting Hill Gate
W11 3QA
71/727-0699
(Tools, powertools)

WEST MIDLANDS

DO IT ALL
Falcon House
The Minories
Dudley
DY2 8PG
38/454-6456 for nearest
store
(Home improvement products)

France

PARIS

BHV
53, rue de Rivoli
75004
42/74-90-00
(Tools and hardware)

Japan

HYOGO

KAIT
984 Myodanicho-Azamaeda
Tarumi-ku, Kobe-shi 655
078/708-2051
(Carpenter's tools)

KANAGAWA

BEAVER TOZAN
191 Itabashi
Odawara-shi 250
0465/23-3611
(Do-it-yourself necessities)

DOIT
2-8-5 Tsumada-Nishi
Atsugi-shi, Kanagawa 243
0462/21-5551
(Do-it-yourself materials)

KYOTO

ASAHI PLAZA
40 Shimotoba-Osadacho
Fushimi-ku 612
075/602-8881
(Do-it-yourself necessities)

NIC HOBBY SHOP
26 Nishikyogoku-
Daimoncho
Ukyo-ku 615
075/313-1330
(Do-it-yourself materials)

TOKYO

NAGASAKIYA HOME
CENTER
1-26-22 Higashi-Hokima
Adachi-ku 121
03/3883-3810
(Do-it-yourself necessities)

SEIYU DAIK
1-8-1 Fukasawa
Setagaya-ku 158
03/3703-8866
(General store for everyday
living)

SHIBUYA LOFT
21-1 Udagawacho
Shibuya-ku 150
03/3462-0111
(Carpenter's tools)

TOHO NICHIYO-DAIKU
CENTER
1-9-1 Tamagawa
Chofu-shi 182
0424/84-2319
(Carpenter's tools)

TOKYU HANDS
MACHIDA
4-1-17 Haramachida
Machida-shi 194
0427/28-2511
(Carpenter's tools)

RESOURCES

36–37 **SCREWS** (from left) screw eye; lead wall
anchor; flathead sheet metal screw;
flathead wood screw; stove bolt; plastic
wall anchor; brass sheet metal screw;
hollow wall anchor; toggle bolt; all from
H. Brickman & Sons

38 **LEVEL,** contractor grade, by Stanley from
Metropolitan Lumber & Hardware;
COMBINATION SQUARE by Starret
from Garrett Wade; **CARPENTER'S
SQUARE** by Johnson from CK & L
Hardware

40 6' folding **WOOD RULE** from Ace
Hardware

41 25' Leverlock **TAPE MEASURE** by Stanley
from H. Brickman & Sons

42 Variable speed **ELECTRIC DRILL**
borrowed from H. Brickman & Sons

43 **HAND DRILL,** Fiskars brand from
Metropolitan Lumber & Hardware

44 Assorted **DRILL BITS** from Spring Street
Hardware

46 (left) **SCRATCH AWL** by Stanley; (right)
CARPENTER'S PENCIL by Dixon; both
from H. Brickman & Sons

49 Blue nylon **TOOL ORGANIZER** for
5-gallon bucket by Busy Pockets from
Metropolitan Lumber & Hardware

BEYOND BASICS

50 Steel **TOOLBOX** from Garrett Wade

52 **VISE-GRIPS** (top) 4" needlenose,
(bottom) 10" curved jaws, both by
Vise-Grip, from H. Brickman & Sons

54 Standard **BLOCK PLANE** by Stanley from
Garrett Wade

55–56 (from left) **COPING SAW** from Garrett
Wade; **NAIL SET** by Stanley from
Metropolitan Lumber & Hardware;
TACK HAMMER by Great Neck from
Metropolitan Lumber & Hardware;
CARPENTER'S MALLET from Garrett
Wade; **CABINET SCREWDRIVER** from
Garrett Wade; **SPOKESHAVE** by Stanley
from Garrett Wade; standard **MARKING
GAUGE** from Garrett Wade

58 **CIRCULAR SAW BLADES** (from top) for
metal; for wood, chrome plated; for
plywood; for masonry; for wood, crosscuts,
fast cuts, miters; for wood, splinter-free
crosscut; all from H. Brickman & Sons

59 **CIRCULAR SAW** by DeWalt from
H. Brickman & Sons

61 12 oz. brass **PLUMB BOB** by General
from H. Brickman & Sons

63 Power **STAPLE GUN** by Black & Decker
from H. Brickman & Sons

64 (left) **MULTI-PLIERS** by Klein Tools from
CK & L Hardware; (right) 7" **WIRE
CUTTER** by Ace Hardware from
H. Brickman & Sons

65 **SOLDERING GUN** by Weller from Metropolitan Lumber & Hardware

66–67 **DIGITAL LEVEL** by Smartlevel from Garrett Wade

68 Various **FASTENERS,** Eve Ashcraft collection

70 **FIVE-IN-ONE TOOL** by Hyde from H. Brickman & Sons

72–73 (top) 1" **WOOD CHISEL** by Stanley from CK & L Hardware; (bottom) **COLD CHISEL** by Dasco Pro from H. Brickman & Sons

74 (from left) 10" **ADJUSTABLE WRENCH** by General Tech; **CLOSED** or **BOX END WRENCH** by Omaha; **OPEN-END WRENCH** by Stanley; all from H. Brickman & Sons

75 10" **ADJUSTABLE WRENCH** by General Tech from H. Brickman & Sons

76 **WORK BELT** and **TOOL HOLDER** by Nicholas from Metropolitan Lumber & Hardware

78 (from top) 4-piece **RATCHET WRENCHES** by Ace Hardware from H. Brickman & Sons; **SOCKET SCREWDRIVER** by Vaco from H. Brickman & Sons ; **SOCKET WRENCH** by Ace Hardware from H. Brickman & Sons; **ALLEN** or **HEX KEY** set by Eklind from Metropolitan Lumber & Hardware

80 Lenox brand **HACKSAW** from Garrett Wade

81 Two-sided ryoba **JAPANESE SAW** from Garrett Wade

82 (clockwise from upper left) **HOSE CLAMP** by Pony from H. Brickman & Sons; **SPRING CLAMP** by Quickgrip from H. Brickman & Sons; **WEB** or **BAND CLAMP,** various sizes, from Metropolitan Lumber & Hardware; **C-CLAMP,** Eve Ashcraft collection

84–85 (from left) **PROPANE TORCH** by Servistar from Metropolitan Lumber & Hardware; **ADJUSTABLE WRENCH** by Channel Lock from H. Brickman & Sons; **STRAP WRENCH** by Ridgid from Metropolitan Lumber & Hardware; **DRAIN AUGER** by Lewisan Products from CK & L Hardware; 14" **PIPE WRENCH** by General Tech from H. Brickman & Sons; **TEFLON TAPE,** PTFE thread seal, from Metropolitan Lumber & Hardware; **HANDLE HACKSAW BLADE** from H. Brickman & Sons

86 (clockwise from upper left) 2" **DUCT TAPE** by Anchor from H. Brickman & Sons; **ELECTRICAL TAPE** from H. Brickman & Sons; **COMBINATION WHETSTONE** from Garrett Wade; **CIRCUIT TESTER** by Gem from H. Brickman & Sons; **CHALK LINE,** Eve Ashcraft collection; **STUD FINDER** by Johnson from H. Brickman & Sons

89 **TOOLBOX** from Garrett Wade; tools from all sources

QUOTES

2 **ANONYMOUS,** *The Penguin Dictionary of Modern Humorous Quotations* (Penguin Books, 1987).

8 **AUSTRALIAN ABORIGINAL SAYING**

11 **MILAN KUNDERA,** *The Columbia Dictionary of Quotations* (Columbia University Press, 1993).

13 **ARTHUR C. CLARKE,** *The Harper Book of Quotations* (HarperCollins, 1993).

15 **DAVE BARRY,** *The Taming of the Screw* (Rodale Press, 1983).

17 **ARTHUR BLOCH,** *The Penguin Dictionary of Modern Humorous Quotations* (Penguin Books, 1987).

20 **WINSTON CHURCHILL,** *Familiar Quotations* (Little, Brown and Company, 1992).

23 **WILLIAM SHAKESPEARE,** *Familiar Quotations* (Little, Brown and Company, 1992).

25 **PAUL R. EHRLICH,** *The Harper Book of Quotations* (HarperCollins, 1993).

28 **TRADITIONAL FOLK SONG**

48 **MONTA CRANE,** *Good Advice,* by William Safire and Leonard Safir (Wings Books, Random House, 1982).

51 **DAVID OWEN,** *The Walls Around Us* (Villard Books, 1991).

66 **HENRY WADSWORTH LONGFELLOW,** "The Building of the Ship," 1850.

72 **MICHELANGELO,** *The Harper Book of Quotations* (HarperCollins, 1993).

77 **THOMAS JEFFERSON,** *Peter's Quotations* (William Morrow, 1977).

79 **DAVE BARRY,** *The Taming of the Screw* (Rodale Press, 1983).

101 **WAYNE WOLF,** Interview.

104 **RALPH WALDO EMERSON,** *International Thesaurus of Quotations* (Harper & Row, Publishers, Inc, 1987).

> "It starts out with a few key pieces—next thing you know you're running down the street with a fistful of dollars screaming after the Snap-On truck like it's going to run out of your favorite flavor."

WAYNE WOLF

ACKNOWLEDGMENTS

A very special thanks to Pow, my grandfather who taught me which tool to use when, I will never forget the smell of your garage, of oil and wood and summer

J.S.

MANUFACTURER & RETAIL RESEARCH	Susan Claire Maloney
QUOTE RESEARCH	Lige Rushing & Kate Doyle Hooper
COPY EDITING	Borden Elniff

AND SPECIAL THANKS TO: Claire Bradley, Tony Chirico, M. Scott Cookson, Henry Daas, Michael Drazen, Deb Freeman, Jane Friedman, Janice Goldklang, Jo-Anne Harrison, Patrick Higgins, Katherine Hourigan, Andy Hughes, Carol Janeway, Barbara Jones-Diggs, Nicholas Latimer, William Loverd, Anne McCormick, Dwyer McIntosh, Sonny Mehta, Anne Messitte, Lan Nguyen, Mitchell Rosenbaum, Alicia Rush, Anne-Lise Spitzer, Robin Swados, Aileen Tse, Shelley Wanger, Cyril Wolf, Amy Zenn.

COMMUNICATIONS

The world has gotten smaller and faster but we still can only be in one place at a time, which is why we are anxious to hear from you. We would like your input on stores and products that have impressed you. We are always happy to answer any questions you have about items in the book, and of course we are interested in feedback about Chic Simple.

Our address is:
84 WOOSTER STREET • NEW YORK, NY 10012
Fax (212)343-9678
Email address: **info@chicsimple.com**
Compuserve number: **72704,2346**

Stay in touch because "The more you know, the less you need."

KIM JOHNSON GROSS & JEFF STONE

TYPE

The text of this book was set in two typefaces: New Baskerville and Futura.
The ITC version of **NEW BASKERVILLE** is called Baskerville, which itself is a facsimile reproduction of types cast from molds made by John Baskerville (1706–1775) from his designs. Baskerville's original face was one of the forerunners of the type style known to printers as the "modern face"—a "modern" of the period A.D. 1800. **FUTURA** was produced in 1928 by Paul Renner (1878–1956), former director of the Munich School of Design, for the Bauer Type Foundry. Futura is simple in design and wonderfully restful in reading. It has been widely used in advertising because of its even, modern appearance in mass and its harmony with a great variety of other modern types.

SEPARATION AND FILM PREPARATION BY
COLOR SYSTEMS
New Britain, Connecticut

PRINTED AND BOUND BY
FRIESEN PRINTERS
Altona, Manitoba, Canada

HARDWARE

Apple Macintosh Quadra 700 and 800 personal computers; APS Technologies Syquest Drives; MicroNet DAT Drive; SuperMac 21" Color Monitor; Radius PrecisionColor Display/20; Radius 24X series Video Board; Hewlett-Packard LaserJet 4, Supra Fax Modem; provided and maintained by Abacus Solutions, New York, New York

SOFTWARE

QuarkXPress 3.3, Adobe Photoshop 2.5.1, Microsoft Word 5.1, FileMaker Pro 2.0, Adobe Illustrator 5.0.1

MUSICWARE

Marvin Gaye *(Anthology)*, Johnny Cash *(American Recordings)*, Greg Brown *(44 & 66)*, Sven Väth *(Accident in Paradise)*, Jimi Hendrix *(Blues)*, Kronos Quartet/Witold Lutoslawski *(String Quartet)*, Nat King Cole *(Just One of Those Things [And More])*, Prince and the New Power Generation, B.B. King *(Blues Summit)*, Dwight Yoakam *(This Time)*, Freni/Pavarotti/Ludwig/Kerns/VPO/Karajan *(Puccini: Madama Butterfly)*, Elmore James *(King of the Slide Guitar)*, Neil Young and Crazy Horse *(Life)*, Various Artists *(Original Motion Picture Soundtrack, Reservoir Dogs)*, Beastie Boys *(Ill Communication)*, Seal *(Seal)*, Thelonious Monk *(The Unique Thelonious Monk)*, Duke Ellington *(The Intimate Ellington)*

"It is very hard to be simple enough to be good."

RALPH WALDO EMERSON